A Teacher of God

by Christine A. Adams

Copyright

Copyright © 2020 Christine A. Adams

All rights reserved. This book or any portion thereof may not be reproduced or used in any manner whatsoever without the express written permission of the publisher except for the use of brief quotations in a book review or scholarly journal.

First Printing: 2020

ISBN: 978-1-7345727-4-2

Published by Hanley-Adams Publishing

Published 09-2020

Christine A. Adams

www.christineaadams.com

Acknowledgement

The source of the words of this book are both **The Course In Miracles and The Holy Bible** combined to help the reader better understand their own place in the spiritual world, and their relationship to God.

Intrigued by the notion that we **all are teachers,** the author, an English teacher, studied these words for many years until she understood the truth and holy wisdom of the concept of **A Teacher of God.**

Today she believes we all teach " what we are and what others are to us." Recorded here, humbly, are not original words but the words and sources that taught her.

Dedication

This book is dedicated to MD Hanley of Hanley-Adams Publishing who tirelessly worked to bring this book to publication.

TABLE OF CONTENTS

A Teacher of God ii

A TEACHER OF GOD 3

THE PROCESS OF GROWTH FOR A TEACHER OF GOD 25

    STEP #1. A Time of "Undoing" 25

    STEP # 2 A Time of "Sorting Out." 26

    STEP # 3 A Time of "Relinquishment." 27

    STEP # 4 A Time of "settling down." 28

    STEP # 5 A Time of "Unsettling." 29

    STEP # 6 A Time of Achievement and Peace. 30

CHARACTERISTICS OF A TEACHER OF GOD 31

    Characteristic # 1 TRUST 31

    Characteristic # 2 HONESTY 32

    Characteristic # 3 TOLERANCE 35

    Characteristic # 4 GENTLENESS 37

    Characteristic # 5 JOY 41

    Characteristic # 6 DEFENSELESSNESS 43

    Characteristic # 7 GENEROSITY 45

    Characteristic # 8 PATIENCE 48

Characteristic # 9 Faithfulness _____ 54

Characteristic # 10 OPEN-MINDEDNESS _____ 56

Also by Christine A. Adams _____ *104*

What is a teacher of God?

In the material world a teacher imparts some special information to a learner, like mathematics or chemistry. In the world of the spirit, the teacher and the learner are the same. As a spiritual teacher you teach what you learn. You become a witness to attest to what you believe.

"For as he thinks in his heart, so is he."

Proverbs 23:7 NKJV

How do spiritual teachers teach?

Spiritual teaching is not done by words alone. Teaching occurs through every situation of your life. You teach others what you are and what they are to you.

"Be an example to them of good deeds of every kind."
Titus 2:7 TLB

A TEACHER OF GOD

Who is a teacher of God?

You are a teacher of God! The question is not whether you will teach for in that there is no choice. Teaching is a constant process which goes on every moment of the day.

"Let everything you do reflect your love of truth."
Titus 2:7 TLB

What do we teach?

The curriculum we set up is determined by what we think we are and what we believe the relationship of others is to us. The self "you believe is real" is what you teach. If you believe you are a vulnerable, limited being you will teach weakness. If you believe you are a powerful spiritual being connected to God, you will teach strength.

"They that wait upon the Lord shall renew their strength; they shall mount up as eagles; and they shall walk and not faint."

Isaiah 40:31 NIV

What is the curriculum of the world?

At some time, most of us followed the world's curriculum trying to teach others we were something we are not. We disown our spiritual selves when we only teach the role of business executive, policeman, nurse or lawyer. These roles are only a small part of our real identity. Until you change your mind about who you are and understand your spiritual identity, you will find yourself teaching a curriculum of the material world which always leads to despair and death.

"For what profit is it to a man if he gains the whole world and loses his own soul? Or what will a man give in exchange for his soul?"

Matthew 16:26 NKJV

What is your spiritual identity?

Your spiritual identity is that you are a child of God. We come from Love, Itself and live in God's love.

"You are from God and have overcome them, because the one who is in you is greater than the one who is in the world."

John 4:4 NIV

You teach as a child of God.

In this role a new perspective emerges. This spiritual perspective enables you to teach joy and hope. When you change your mind about who you are, you become a teacher of God. Now you're learning becomes complete through your teaching.

"I have told you this so that my joy may be in you and that your joy may be complete"

John 15:11 NIV

A teacher of God is anyone who wishes to be one.

Without teachers of God, there would be little hope of salvation. The worlds of sin and death would seem too real. This book is a manual for teachers of God. The calling is there for anyone who wishes to recognize it.

"The joy of the Lord is your strength."
Nehemiah 8:10 KJV

The great paradox of suffering.

Many times, people say they "never know who they are" until they are stripped of all worldly roles and possessions. For example, the dying cancer patient can teach us how to live. Great understanding of the spiritual self can come through great adversity.

"Then you will call, and the Lord will answer; you will cry for help, and he will say: Here I am ..."

Isaiah 58:9 NIV

What is our mission?

It is our mission to become spiritually perfect here, so as we teach perfection over and over again, in many ways, we learn it.

"Then you will know the truth, and the truth will set you free."

John 8:22 NIV

What are the qualifications of a teacher of God?

The qualifications to become a teacher of God are simple. First, somehow, somewhere you made a deliberate choice not to see your own interest apart from someone else's interest. Then the path became clear.

"Learn to put aside your own desires so that you will become patient and godly."

2 Peter 1:6 TLB

A Light in Darkness

It is as if a light has entered the darkness, A single light is enough. The light comes when you make the choice not to see your own interest apart from someone else's and you enter an agreement with God.

"For thou art my lamp, O Lord; and the Lord illuminates my darkness."
2 Samuel 22:29 AKJV

Where do teachers come from?

Teachers come from all over the world. From all religions and from no religion. A call is sent and the teachers answer. Many hear the call but few answer. In time we all will answer the call but it may take a long time. When a teacher answers the call, time is saved.

"And though the Lord give you the bread of adversity and the water of affliction, yet your Teacher will not hide himself any more, and your eyes shall see your Teacher."

Isaiah 30:20 NIV

What kind of course does the teacher teach?

The form of the course varies greatly as do the teaching aides. However, the contents of the course never change. Its central theme is " You are God's Child. You are innocent. You are saved."

"Be imitators of God, therefore, as dearly loved children."
Ephesians 5:1 NIV

How is the lesson taught?

The lesson of love can be taught by action, or thought, by words or soundlessly, in any language, in any place, time or manner. By answering the call to teach, you have found your salvation and the salvation of the world. In your rebirth is the world reborn.

"... let us love one another, for love comes from God. Everyone who loves has been born of God and knows God. Whoever does not love does not know God, because God is love."

1 John 4:38 NIV

Who are the pupils?

Certain pupils have been assigned to each of God's teachers and they will begin to look for that teacher as soon as He has answered the call to teach. The pupils were chosen for the teacher because the form of the curriculum that he teaches is best for them, according to their level of understanding.

"I will instruct you and teach you in the way you should go; I will counsel you and watch over you."

Psalms 32:8 NIV

The right moment comes!

Once the teacher has chosen to fulfill her role, the pupils are ready to fulfill theirs. When the teacher is ready to learn, the opportunities to teach will be provided for her.

"To everything there is a season, a time for every purpose under heaven."

Ecclesiastes 3:1 NKJV

_I_n the right time and place a teaching- learning situation begins.

The pupil will come at the right time and to the right place which was pre-ordained in some ancient instant. When teacher and pupil come together a teaching-learning situation begins.

"Come to me and I will answer you and tell you great and unsearchable things you do not know."

Jeremiah 33:3 NIV

What is a teaching-learning situation?

In the teaching-learning situation, each one learns that giving and receiving are the same. The learner becomes a teacher of God himself, for he has made the one decision that gave his teacher to him. He has seen in another the same interests as his own.

"Ask and you shall receive, that your joy be full."
John 16:26,27 INAB

The goal is a holy relationship.

Each teaching-learning situation involves a different relationship at the beginning, although the ultimate goal is always the same to make the relationship a holy one - One in which both see each other as one, as innocent children of God. There is no one from whom a teacher cannot learn and no one whom he cannot teach.

"For you were once darkness, but now you are in the light in the Lord. Walk as children of light.'

Ephesians 5:8 CEV

There are no coincidences!

There are no coincidences. We will meet those who are there for us to have the potential for a "holy relationship".

"May his miracles have a deep and permanent effect upon you lives!"

Deuteronomy 4:9 TLB

Some encounters seem by chance.

Sometimes, we enter a teaching-learning situation in a very casual encounter--a chance meeting of two strangers. Even in these brief meetings, it is possible for two people to lose sight of separate interests and set up a learning- teaching situation.

"All these are inspired by one and the same Spirit, who apportions to each one individually as he wills."

1 Corinthians 12:11 RSV

You learn from all encounters.

You learn as much as you need from each "holy instant", from each teaching-learning situation, that you need to know at that time. Sometimes you enter into a more substantial relationship and separate after a while. You have learned what you need to know at this time. Perhaps, you will meet again.

"You my brothers, were called to be free ... serve one another in love."

Galatians 5:13 NIV

Some teaching-learning situations are lifelong.

Some teaching-learning situations are lifelong. In these situations, a chosen learning partner presents the other with unlimited opportunities for learning. In these relationships, the opportunity for a holy relationship is present and the perfect lesson can be learned.

"And over all these virtues put on love, which binds them all together in perfect unity."
Colossians 26 3:14 (NKJV)

THE PROCESS OF GROWTH FOR A TEACHER OF GOD

STEP #1. A Time of "Undoing"

First, a teacher of God must go through a time of undoing. It seems like there is great loss because we have not yet come to believe that what we are losing has no great value. We resist some changes in our external circumstances and we can't seem to make the spiritual shift internally. Finally, we come to understand that these changes are helpful to us spiritually.

'If anyone is in Christ, he is a new creation;

the old has gone, the new has come.

2 Corinthians 5:17 NIV

STEP # 2 A Time of "Sorting Out."

Next, the teacher of God begins a time of "sorting out." Once the teacher has learned the changes are helpful, she must decide all things on the basis of whether they increase that helpfulness or hinder it. Most things she valued before now hinder her. Finally, however she will come to know that all things - events, encounters, and circumstances are helpful.

"Each one should retain the place in life that the Lord assigned to Him and to which God has called him."

1 Corinthians 7:17 NIV

Step # 3 A Time of "Relinquishment."

In a period of "relinquishment", the teacher of God gives up the valueless. When she actually relinquishes what she formerly valued, she finds a lightheartedness. Thus, as she gives up what she thought she valued, she finds a gift bestowed on her.

"There are different gifts, but the same spirit. All these are the work of one and the same Spirit, and he gives them to each one just as he determines."

I Corinthians 12:4,11

STEP # 4 A Time of "settling down."

In a time of settling down there is a quiet time when the teacher of God rests. Now she consolidates her learning and values what she has learned. She rests and gathers mighty companions to go with her from this place.

"The wisdom that comes from heaven is first of all pure; then peace-loving, considerate, submissive, full of mercy and good fruit, impartial and sincere."

James 3:17 NIV

STEP # 5 A Time of "Unsettling."

Now after a time of rest, there is a time of "unsettling." Suddenly there is realization that the teacher of God did not know what was valuable and valueless. She still does not know the difference in every case. She must lay judgment aside and ask only for what is needed in each circumstance.

"I am the Lord your God, who teaches you to profit, who leads you in the way you should go."

Isaiah 48:17 RSV

STEP # 6 A Time of Achievement and Peace.

Finally, in the time of achievement, all learning is consolidated. Now what was seen as loss becomes gain, to be counted on in al emergencies as well as in tranquil times. True peace is the result, the outcome of honest learning.

"For God is not a God of confusion, but of peace."
1 Corinthians 14:33 RSV

CHARACTERISTICS OF A TEACHER OF GOD

Characteristic # 1 TRUST

The first characteristic, trust, provides a foundation helping the teachers to function in the world. Teachers of God trust in the world because they have learned that the world is not governed by its own laws but by a power greater than the world. It is that power that keeps them safe. Their trust in all things is in God.

"Trust in the Lord with all your heart, lean not on your understanding; in all ways acknowledge Him, and He shall direct your path,"

Proverbs 3:56 NKJV

Characteristic # 2 HONESTY

All other traits of God's teachers rest on trust. Only the trusting can afford honesty, for only they can see its value. Honesty doesn't apply to what we say. Honesty means consistency. When there is nothing you say that contradicts what you think or do, when no thought opposes any other thought, when no act belies your word. You are truly honest.

"Let everything you do reflect your love of truth."

Titus 2:7 TLB

Peace comes through honesty.

The peace of mind that teachers of God ultimately experience is largely due to their perfect honesty. No one who is at one with himself can conceive of conflict. Self-deception brings conflict – self-deception is dishonesty.

"Make every effort to keep the unity of the Spirit through the bond of peace.
Ephesians 4:3 NIV

A teacher of God will succeed.

A teacher of God will always succeed because they never do their will alone. They choose for all mankind, for all the world and all things in it – for themselves and God. How could they not succeed? They choose in perfect honesty, sure of their choice as of themselves.

"If God be for us, who can be against us?"
Romans 8:31 NIV

Characteristic # 3 TOLERANCE

God's teachers do not judge. To judge is to be dishonest because by judging you assume a position you do not have. Judgment implies you have been deceived in your view of others. If you are deceived in your view of others, you are deceived in your view of yourself.

"Judge not that you be not judged. For with the judgment, you pronounce you will be judged, and the measure you give will be the measure you get."

Matthew 7: 1,2 RSV

Judgment implies a lack of trust.

Judgment of others implies a lack of trust and trust is the basis of the teacher of god's whole thought system. Let trust go and all the learning is gone. Without judgment all things are equally acceptable. All men are brothers, all women, sisters. None stands apart. Judgment destroys honesty and shatters trust. No teacher of God can judge and hope to learn.

"Then let us no more pass judgment on one another, but rather decide never to put a stumbling block or hindrance in the way of a brother."

Romans 14:13 RSV

Characteristic # 4 GENTLENESS

The third characteristic of teachers of God is gentleness. Intentional harming of others is impossible for all God's teachers. They can neither harm nor be harmed. Harm is the outcome of judgment. It is a dishonest act that follows a dishonest thought. When you put a verdict of guilty on a brother, or sister, you put it on yourself.

"Be beautiful inside, in your hearts, with the lasting charm of a quiet spirit that is so precious to God."

1 Peter 3:4 TLB

Harm through judgment is negative.

When harm is caused through judgment, that harmfulness completely obliterates the teacher's function from his awareness. It will make him defensive, fearful, angry and suspicious. The Holy Spirit's lesson cannot be learned when there is harmfulness. No gain can come from it.

"Agree with God, and be at peace; in this way good will come to you."

Job 22:21 NRSV

God's teachers are totally gentle.

Teachers of God need the strength of gentleness. Who would choose the weakness that comes from harming another through judgment when they could choose the unfailing, all-encompassing and limitless strength of gentleness.

"Be humble and gentle. Be patient with each other, making allowance for each other's faults because of your love."

Ephesians 4:2 TLB

There is power in gentleness.

The power of God's teachers lies in their gentleness. Thus do they join their thoughts with God who is their source. And so, their will becomes one with God's and they make decisions on the freedom of that oneness.

"But the fruit of the Spirit is ... gentleness."
Galatians 5:22,23 NIV

Characteristic # 5 JOY

Joy is the inevitable result of gentleness. Gentleness means that fear is now impossible, and what could come to interfere with joy? The open hands of gentleness are always filled. The gentle have no pain. They cannot suffer. So why would they not be joyous? They are sure they are beloved, and they are safe.

"He will fill your mouth with laughter and your lips with shouts of joy."
Job 8:21 AKJV

Gratitude comes out of joy!

As sure as grief goes with attack, joy goes with gentleness. Joy is God's teacher's song of thanks. God's teachers trust in Him. They hold His gifts and follow His way, because God's voice directs them in all things.

"I have told you this so that my joy may be in you and that joy may be complete

John 15:11 NIV

Characteristic # 6   DEFENSELESSNESS

God's teachers have learned how to be simple. They have no illusions that need defense against the truth. They do not make themselves a God trying to "create " themselves. Their joy comes from understanding who created them. Does What God create need defense?

"If God be for us, who can be against us?"

Romans 8:31 NIV

There is No Danger.

The more grotesque the illusion, the fiercer and more powerful its defense seems to be. A teacher of God knows that once you look past illusions nothing is there. The teacher of God learns this lesson slowly at first and then faster as trust increases. Some believe that danger comes when defenses are laid down. Defenselessness is safety. It is peace. It is joy. It is God.

"Your attitude should be the same as Christ Jesus."
Philippians 4:7 NIV

Characteristic # 7 GENEROSITY

The term generosity has special meaning to the teacher of God. It is not the usual meaning of the word. The meaning must be learned very carefully. Like all other characteristics this one rests on trust for without trust no one can be generous. To the world "giving away" means "giving up." To the teacher f God, it means giving away in order to keep. It is the exact opposite of the world's thinking.

"Remembering the words of the Lord Jesus, for he himself said, "It is more blessed to give than to receive."

Acts 20:35 NKJV

Giving Is Receiving

The teacher of God is generous out of self-interest. But this reference to self is not the Self of which the world speaks. The teacher of God does not want anything he cannot give away because he realizes it would be valueless to him. What would he want it for? He will only lose because of it. He could not gain.

"Do not conform any longer to the pattern of the world, but be transformed by the renewing of your mind."

Romans 12:2 NIV

Keep only The Things of God

A teacher of God does not seek what he only could keep because it guarantees loss. He does not want to suffer. Why should he insure himself of pain? But he does want to keep for himself all things that are of God, and therefore made for Him. These he can give away in real generosity, protecting them forever for himself.

"Ask and you shall receive; that your joy be full."
John 16:26,27 IAAB

Characteristic # 8 PATIENCE

When we are certain of the outcome of anything, we can afford to wait and do it without anxiety. Patience is a natural attribute to a teacher of God.

"Learn to put aside your own desires so that you will become patient and godly, gladly letting God have his way with you."

2 Peter 1:6 TLB

There is a Time For All Things

The timing of things does not bother the teacher of God because everything is in the "right time.' The time will be as right as the answer is.

"For everything there is a season, and a time for every matter under heaven.
Ecclesiastes 3:1 RSV

The Past Is Gone.

Sometimes we get caught up in a very dangerous pattern of rehashing the past. We say 'what if" this had happened or that had not happened. The truth is the past holds nothing that did not serve the world and the people to which it happened. The past simply is. Now what?

'No matter what happens, always be thankful, for this is God's will for you who belong to Christ Jesus."

I Thessalonians 5:18 TLB

Out of Pain Comes Learning

Perhaps it is not understood at the time but the teacher of God becomes willing to reconsider all past decisions especially those that cause pain. Out of that pain came some learning, some benefit to the world that can only be seen in retrospect. There is a purpose for all things. even pain.

"A time to weep, and a time to laugh; a time to mourn, and a time to dance;"

` Ecclesiastes 3: 4 RSV

Patience Comes Back To Trust

There is always a defining moment when we are asked to say, "What is the lesson here?" What am I being taught? The teacher and the learner are inextricably joined in the learning process even when the lesson is not clear. Trusting in the outcome of that process takes patience.

'Love is patient; love is kind. It does not insist on its own way."

I Corinthians 13:45 NRSV

Replace Fear With Faith

A teacher of God learns to replace fear with faith. Whenever they sense fear within themselves, they go back to God. A lack of faith could indicate they are impatient with some outcome that they can't understand, or are fearful of the future. A teacher of God trusts patiently!

"Whether you turn to the right or to the left, your ears will hear a voice behind you saying, "This is the way ; walk in it."

Isaiah 30:21 RSV

Characteristic # 9 Faithfulness

The extent of the teacher of God's faithfulness is the measure of his advancement. Faithfulness is the teacher of God's trust in the word of God--to set all thing right, not some, but all. Faithfulness requires we give up everything, in faith, to God.

"A faithful man will be richly blessed."
Proverbs 28:20 NIV

True Faithfulness Is Consistent

True faithfulness does not deviate. Being consistent it is wholly honest. Being unswerving, it is full of trust. Being based in fearlessness. it is gentle. Being centered, it is joyous. And being confident, it is tolerant. Faithfulness confines within it, the other attributes of God's teachers.

"Let love and faithfulness never leave you; ...
and write them on the tablet of your heart."
Proverbs 3:3 NIV

Characteristic # 10 OPEN-MINDEDNESS

Open-mindedness comes from a lack of judgment. Judgment closes the mind of anyone against himself. Open-mindedness invites him in. Open-mindedness allows Christ's image to be extended to him. Only the open-minded can be at peace, because they see the reason for peace.

"Judge not that you be not judged.
For with the judgment, you pronounce you will be judged,
and the measure you give will be the measure you get."
Matthew 7:1 RSV

*F*orgiveness is the key.

The open-minded teacher has let go of all things that would prevent forgiveness. By abandoning the world, it is restored to him. Restored in a glorious newness. The newness of open-mindedness is a change he could never have conceived. Nothing is as it was formerly.

'Bear with each other and forgive whatever grievances you may have against one another. Forgive as the Lord forgave you."

Colossians 3:13 NIV

Freedom in Forgiveness

All things are welcoming because the threat is gone to those who are open-minded. The final goal of the curriculum is achieved in forgiveness which is beyond all learning.

"...forgive and you will be forgiven..."
Luke 37 RSV

Know the truth.

It is the function of the teacher of God to bring true learning to the world. Actually, it is the "unlearning' that they bring. Teachers of God bring complete forgiveness to the world. Blessed are the bringers of salvation.

"Then you will know the truth, and the truth will set you free."
John 8:22 NIV

What is the function of a teacher of God?

Sickness is of the mind not of the body. Sickness is a faulty problem-solving approach; it is a decision. The teacher of God comes to those who do not understand what healing is. A teacher of God does not directly heal the sick but reminds them of the remedy God has already given them. The teacher heals by giving away what God has given them.

"Heal the sick, raise the dead...."
Matthew 10:8 RSV

Miracles will happen.

The teacher of God is a miracle worker because he gives the gifts he receives. Yet he must first accept these gifts as his own. By accepting healing, he gives it. Doubt not the gift and it is impossible to doubt its result. The is the certainty that gives God's teachers the power to be miracle workers, for they have put their trust in God.

'Him whom thou blessest is blessed."

Numbers 22:6 KJV

A change in attitude.

Changes in attitude are the first step in the new teacher of God's training, She learns not that she should not judge but that she cannot judge. In order to judge anything in the right way, one would have to be fully aware of an inconceivably wide range of things; past, present and to come. One would have to be capable of recognizing in advance all the effects on everyone and everything involved. Who is in the position to do this?

"Come to me and I will answer you and tell you great and unsearchable things you do not know."

Jeremiah 33:3 NIV

The Teacher of God lays down judgment.

A teacher of God recognizes God's presence in his life. God's judgment is perfect. God knows all the facts; past, present , and to come. God knows the effect of His judgment on everyone involved. He is wholly fair to everyone. The teacher of God lays down judgment with a sense of gratitude.

"He is my refuge and my fortress; my God; in Him I trust."

Psalm 91:2 KJV

How should the teacher of God spend his day?

There is no set program for any day. A teacher of God will be told all that she should be, this day and every day. Those who have come to her to be her pupils will find her so they can learn the lessons for the day together. No one is sent without a learning goal already set--one which can be learned that very day.

'And know that all things work together for good to them that love God, to them who are called according to his purpose."

Romans 8:28 KJV

Starting and ending the day with God.

In general, it is well to start the day by spending time with God. It is always possible to begin again if things go wrong. AS soon as possible after waking, take quiet time with God and again in the evening set your mind into a pattern of rest by thoughts of peace. Close your eyes and thank God.

"My voice thou shalt hear in the morning, O Lord, in the morning will I direct my people unto thee, and will look up."

Psalm 5:3 KJV

How is peace found?

No one can fail to find it who seeks it. God's peace can never come where anger is. Anger denies that peace exists. A teacher of God sees that anger is not justified in any way in any circumstance. Therefore, forgiveness is the necessary condition for finding the peace of God.

"Let not the sun go down on your wrath."
Ephesians 4:26 KJV

Prayers of the heart.

Prayer is the motivating factor in healing. What you ask for with prayers of the heart; you receive. The prayer of the heart does not ask for concrete things. It requests experiences that are hoped for. The prayer for things of the world will bring experiences of the world.

"For everyone who asks receives, and he who seeks finds, and to him who knocks it will be opened."

Luke 11:10 RSV

How does a teacher of God communicate?

Many pupils will be reached through words because they are unable to hear I silence. The teacher of God has learned to use words in a new way. He lets his words be chosen for him. The teacher of God accepts the words when they are offered him, and gives as he receives. These words are wiser than his own. He listens and hears and speaks.

"When they deliver you up, do not be anxious how you are to speak or what you are to say; for what you are to say will be given to you in that hour."

Matthew 10:19 RSV

Ask in the Name of Jesus Christ.

The name of Jesus Christ is the symbol that stands for a love that is not of this world. Remembering the name of Jesus Christ is to give thanks for all the gifts God has given you. and gratitude to God becomes the way in which He is remembered. Love cannot be far behind a grateful heart.

"I have no silver and gold, but I give you what I have; in the name of Jesus Christ of Nazareth walk."

Acts 3;6 RSV

Jesus leads the way.

Jesus went beyond the farthest reaches of learning. We learn the lesson of salvation through his learning. Why would we choose to start again, when he made the journey for us? He will take us with him, for he did not go alone. We were with him then, as we are now. Jesus has come to answer our questions--with God's answer. Teachers of God teach with him for he is with us , he is always with us.

"Jesus said to her , 'I am the resurrection and the life; he who believes in me, though he die, yet shall he live, and whoever lives and believes in me shall never die.' "

John 11:25 RSV

Dear God,

You are the author of all life.

Let me set my sights high enough;

Let me see that I am not a limited

Woman, in a limited body, but

your child, a child of God.

How easy it is to let the world

Tell me what I am . How easy it is

To get distracted but things which have

Little meaning to me. Pull me back

O, Lord to you and the real me.

Lord,

Let me keep a special place in my heart, A place that is pure, a place free from confusion and fear, a place where love can abide with you, my God of Love.

Your joy will be in me "is what you

tell me. All I need to do is hear your
voice and accept the happiness in my world.
Let me rejoice in the song of my life.
Dear God, let me hear your voice calling me.

The Truth of what I am is not for words

to speak or describe. Yet my words can

demonstrate my function as God's child,

and speak of this and teach it too.

I need exemplify God's word in me.

Let me teach what you have taught me;

Let me sing your praises in my actions; in my work; and in my thoughts. Let me live the calling you have chosen for me.

Whatever adversity comes my way,

let me be prepared. Take away my fear

of death, of pain, of suffering.

Let me live, unafraid, in your love

each day.

When I can see only my own will,

only my own desires, help me to hear others
when they speak, to listen with a heart
full of compassion, with tears ready
to spill over, ready to wash away all
differences.

Dear Lord,

Help me to put aside my judgements,

my strong condemnations of others

which are really condemnation of myself.

Let me know your love so that I may teach it.

I **never know what the lesson**

may be, or where you will take

me to learn my truth. Let me be

a willing partner in love with you,

O God, give me the strength to

carry on, and not to question your word.

As your plan unfolds, I see the power

Of your infinite wisdom. Keep my mind

open to the mystery of life when I can't

understand. Keep me in faith

when I am blind to my direction.

As your plan unfolds, I see the power

Of your infinite wisdom, Keep my mind
open to the mystery of life when I can't
understand. Keep me in faith
when I am blind to my direction.

Make all my relationship[s holy, O God

Let me see all I meet as I see myself,

a holy child of God.

Open the eyes of my mind to "holy instants."

Help me to be present in the moments of
all time so that I may learn from situations
that are devised by a mind greater than
my own. Let me understand that
you are the mind which, I think.

As things change around me

Let me hold onto the permanence of you
my God. Let me go back to the home
in my heart where you dwell, to the peace
that lives there, to the completeness
of your love. Let me be still a moment.

As I sort out my life experiences,

guide me, dear Lord, because I can never see all there is to see. It will be enough to understand all things work together for good for those who love you.

Through all the stages of learning

there will be questions without answers,
confusion with the answers that appear;
and sometimes an absence of the question
itself. Pull me through the stages of my
learning, dear Lord. Without You,
there is no direction.

The only real gifts are those given to me

by you, God. I will freely give those away

So that I may keep them, just as God has

Freely given them to me.

I **need no defense against the world.**

When you created me, you gave me all that
I need to be safe in the world. I do not want to live
in fear, armed with useless defenses that
only serve as means to attack others.

*L*ord, show me the power of a more gentle manner. Lead me to words that cheer and soothe others, never chiding or badgering them. Help me to teach love in a gentle way.

Dear God,

My joy is complete in you. All I have to do is accept that happiness is your will for me, I can choose to be happy this moment!

When I am quick to judge, let me hold back

that judgement, O Lord. Let me quickly

remember that judgment of another

condemns me.

Let me set a guard over my actions

and my words so that what I say does

not contradict what I do. Help me

to be true to the values I speak

in your name, Jesus.

*L*et me trust in you O, Lord.

In your infinite wisdom,
In your gentle love,
And in your strength which is
Successful in all things.

In quiet let me look on the world,

Which reflects your thoughts.
Let me remember you are the
creator of this world and I will see
its gentleness.

A special blessing come to me today.

A blessing from God. I will give this day to Him, and there will be no fear. This day will be given to Love.

Help me not to interfere in the work

you would have me do this day, O God.

Let my mind be quiet to recieve3 the

thoughts You offer me. Guide me

along the quiet path that leads to You.

*F*ather, the peace of Christ is given us,

because it is Your Will that we be saved.
Help us today to accept, your gift, and judge
it not. For it has come to us to save us
from our judgement of ourselves.

We spend this day together, you and I.

And all the world joins with us in our song of joy and thankfulness to Him who gave salvation to, who set us free. We are restored to peace and holiness.

References:

A Course In Miracles, Tiburon, CA: **Foundation For Inner Peace**, 1975.

Louise L. Hay, **The Power Is Within You**, Santa Monica, CA: Hay House, Inc., 1991

Gay Hendricks and Kathlyn Hendricks, **Conscious Loving,** New York, NY: Bantam Books, 1990.

Hugh Prather, **This Is The Place Where You Are Not Alone — Reflections On A Course In Miracles**, New York, NY: Doubleday, 1980.

Marianne Williamson, **A Return To Love — Reflections and Principles of A Course In Miracles**, **New York, NY: Harper Collins Publishers, 1992.**

Gerald G. Jampolsky, **Teach Only Love** , New York, NY: Bantam Books, 1983.

Frances Vaughn and Roger Walsh, **Accept This Gift,** New York, NY: Putnam Publishing Group, **1983**

Tara Singh, **A Course In Miracles — A Gift For All Mankind,** Los Angeles, CA: Life Action Press, **1992.**

Joan Borysenko, Ph.D. **Guilt Is The Teacher — Love Is The Lesson,** New York, NY: Warner Books, 1990.

Jampolsky, Gerald G., M.D. **Love Is Letting Go Of Fear,** Celestial Arts, Berkeley, CA: 1979.

Jampolsky, Gerald G., M.D. Out Of The Darkness Into The Light, New York, NY: Bantam Books, 1989.

Gerald G. Jampolsky, M.D. Goodbye To Guilt, New York, NY: Bantam Books, 1985.

Peck, M. Scott, M.D. The Road Less Traveled, New York, NY: Simon and Schuster, 1978.

Prather, Hugh. This Is A Place Where You Are Not Alone — Reflections On A Course In Miracles, New York, NY: Doubleday, 1980.

Singh, Tara. Love Holds No Grievances. Foundation For Life Action, Los Angeles, CA: 1986.

The Song Of Prayer: Prayer, Forgiveness, Healing. Foundation For Inner Peace, Tiburon, CA: 1978.

Vaughn, Frances and Roger Walsh. Accept This Gift. Putnam Publishing Group, New York, NY: 1983.

Vaughn, Frances and Roger Walsh. **A Gift Of Peace: Selections From A Course In Miracles**. Putnam Publishing Group, New York, NY: 1986.

Thich Nhat Hanh, **Peace In Every Step**, New York, NY: Bantam Books, 1991

Marianne Williamson, **A Year of Miracles: Devotions and Reflections**, New York, NY: Harper One, 2015

Also by Christine A. Adams

ABC's of Grief - A Handbook for Survivors

Let Go and Let God

Living in Love

Summer of Love

Holy Relationships

Claiming Your Own Life

School Factory

Love, Infidelity, and Sexual Addiction

Gratitude Therapy

One Day At A Time

Learning To Be A Good Friend

Happy To Be Me

Worry, Worry, Go Away

God Made Us One By One

Watch for more at Christine A. Adams's site.

www.ingramcontent.com/pod-product-compliance
Lightning Source LLC
Chambersburg PA
CBHW081231080526
44587CB00022B/3895